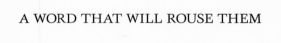

A WORD THAT WILL ROUSE THEM

A WORD THAT WILL ROUSE THEM

Reflections on the Ministry of Reader

by Aelred R. Rosser

Liturgy Training Publications

Liturgy Training Publications
1800 North Hermitage Avenue
Chicago IL 60622-1101
1-800-933-1800 FAX 1-800-933-7094

This book was edited by David A. Lysik. Deborah Bogaert was the pro-
duction editor. It was designed by Kerry Perlmutter and typeset by
Mark Hollopeter in Veljovic. Printed by Darwill Press. The front cover
design and illustrations are the work of Katherine Weingart-Wolff.

Library of Congress Cataloging-in-Publications Data
Rosser, Aelred R. (Aelred Robert)
   A word that will rouse them : reflections on the ministry of reader
/ by Aelred R. Rosser.
       p. cm.
   Includes bibliographical references.
   1. Lay readers — Catholic Church. 2. Word of God (Theology)
3. Catholic Church — Liturgy. I. Title.
BX1915.R67 1995
264'.34 — dc20   95-11671
                                                            CIP

ISBN 1-56854-028-0
ROUSE

My earliest memories of the words of the Bible date back to about 1950. They remain quite vivid. The words came thundering from the pulpit and from the glistening countenance of a fundamentalist Baptist preacher who was acutely aware that he was engaged with a very powerful force. The words rolled down the aisles of our tiny country church like great boulders, threatening to crush us mercilessly. "Arise, go thy way; thy faith hath made thee whole," was as terrifying as "Get thee hence, Satan." The great God of judgment spoke both. But the terror was cleansing; the experience was empowering because it fulfilled my expectations. In the exalted strangeness of the King James translation, these words washed over me like a weekly baptism, purging away any notion that God was hard to know or beyond my experience. No, God was evidently and horribly real. The preacher saw to that by proclaiming God's words with the thunder and smoke they deserved. In short, he did what proclamation is supposed to do — he made God present. And how!

1960: A decade later would find me newly converted to Catholicism and hearing the words of the Bible in a very different setting: serving at the steps to the altar long before dawn, listening to the nearly inaudible words of the gospel as a heavily-robed monk murmured them softly in Latin. The gentle undulations of the strange language and the hushed atmosphere of the dimly lighted abbey church enveloped me in an awed reverence. There was no doubt in my mind that God was truly present in those words, heavily veiled and appropriately distanced. Familiar formulas fulfilled my expectations. *"In illo tempore, Jesus dixit discipulis suis. . . ."* God was very near, though mysterious and elusive; the faint echoes of mighty deeds recorded in sacred scripture issued from the priest's lips in words too sacred to be immediately grasped, too revered to be uttered in everyday language — compelling, wrenching and transforming in the power of their ancient beauty. Later that day I would follow the translation in my English missal as these words were proclaimed again — at the High Mass, clothed in the solemnity of a hypnotic chant.

1970: Another decade, and yet another experience of God's words, now spoken by neither a preacher nor a priest but by a lay person. The church is in the initial flush of sweeping liturgical reforms, and all the words are in English, in the vernacular. The reader is a young man of great faith. He has made these words his own and now proclaims them with friendly familiarity. There is no brimstone in his delivery, but there is warmth as he accents the text with hand gestures and a variety of facial expressions. There is no over-awed reverence but rather unmistakable earnestness; there is directness, a personal involvement in the message and love for the service he is performing. I am struck by the immediacy of these familiar words, for they have been endowed with intimacy by the reader. He has made the word seem accessible, comfortable, easy, almost matter-of-fact — a practical guide by which to live in harmony with my neighbor and my God.

Three very different experiences over a span of only 20 years. Three very different approaches to the timeless tradition of communicating the word of God. And each of the three seemed appropriate as I experienced it. The great God of judgment, the "wholly other" God of mystery and the gentle God of loving kindness each fulfilled my expectations and left me satisfied that the good news of Jesus continued to fill the world.

After many subsequent years of wrestling with the effective proclamation of the word, each of the three now seems inadequate. The thunder of the preacher's certainty acknowledged God's sovereignty over a puny and sinful world, not only forming my view of Christian life but limiting it as well. There was little room for wonder. The search for faith was soon over in a world neatly projected in black and white. Questions were routine. Answers were easy. Proclamation was confirmation, pure and simple, of the all-seeing presence of the God of righteousness who had made the divine will simple and clear. Obedience to that will was the crux of the experience.

The strangeness of the priest's chant echoed the cosmic mystery of God's "otherness." It created a world of its own, very different from my daily experience — as, indeed, I felt it should be. It proved efficacious precisely because it drew me apart from the mundane and into the spiritual — where God was. There was little need to mesh these two worlds. Indeed, they were at odds, the one providing refuge from the other and thereby fulfilling its purpose. By drawing me into the world of "the other," the exalted proclamation transported me into God's presence and away from the world of daily life.

The warmth of the young man's informal earnestness seemed just right for the seventies. It made the loving kindness of God very personal, very accessible, and above all, relevant to modern times.

No magic or mystery here. God was made present in the smiling face of my neighbor. Again, because my thinking about God had changed, my expectations of the proclaimed word were fulfilled.

It troubles me that each of these three very different approaches to the proclamation of the word — over a relatively short span of time — seemed appropriate when I experienced them. It troubles me even more that none of the three seems adequate to me now. Did a certain style of liturgical proclamation re-form my expectation every ten years and then fulfill it? Can we speak of a timeless approach to proclamation that is always relevant and effective? To what degree is the mode of proclamation determined by myriad specific times and places?

Most troubling of all is the question that haunts me now in the mid-1990s, more than 30 years after Vatican II and after almost as many years of teaching, coaching and writing for those who serve the People of God as readers. *Is the ministry of reader achieving its purpose?*

In reflecting on this question I want to address myself to those who now serve as readers as well as to those who may be called to this ministry in the future. Anyone who formulates this kind of question has some notion that there is at least a tentative answer. It is no different with me. But what I offer here are truly reflections, not judgments or pronouncements. If they contribute something to the discourse that deals with a community's ongoing search for viable ritual forms to express its faith, then I shall be satisfied . . . for the moment, at least!

*The Lord G*OD *has given me a well-trained tongue,*
That I may know how to speak to the weary
a word that will rouse them.

Isaiah 50:4

Introduction

The God who is inscrutable and sovereign is also the Good Shepherd. The God of cosmic mystery became flesh in human form and washed Peter's feet. The God who is nearer to us than we are to ourselves is also greater than our hearts.

How is one to proclaim God's word to the assembly, not just adequately but compellingly and authentically? Is it possible to do full justice to the word and to the God who is revealed in it? Yes, it is possible if we understand the immensity of what we are called to do: if we know that God's *word* is God's *work* and will accomplish the purpose for which it is sent; if we believe in the power of the word; and if we become true servants of the word, filled with faith in its power — true lovers of the word, allowing it to be greater than our hearts.

When we are fully engaged with the word of God, we become sensitive to its vastness and its immediacy. We sense — and we communicate — the timelessness of the word as well as its relevance to every moment of human life. Our objective then becomes to allow the word to work its effect — not to interpret it, adapt it or modernize it (how can we modernize the timeless?) but to serve it. Genuine ministry is always humble service.

When we take on the role of ministry in its fullness, much must be given up. John the Baptist is our model here. He had to disappear so that the Messiah could appear: "He must increase; I must decrease" (John 3:30), the Baptist said. And another John said of the Baptist, "He was not the light, but came to testify to the light" (John 1:8). That is the most we can do as ministers of the word. We can proclaim it well and bear witness to it faithfully and with all the communication skills available to human effort, but we remain very much aware that our proclamation is not the word and that our ministry is not the word. The word is God's work of saving love. The word *is* God.

There is comfort and encouragement in knowing this. There is comfort in realizing that, ultimately, the effectiveness of the word is neither in doubt nor our responsibility. There is encouragement in realizing that God has entrusted us with the proclamation of a word whose effectiveness is guaranteed.

Does this imply that the effort and role of the reader are minimal? Of course not. In fact, just the opposite is true: Readers who acknowledge that they are in service to the word will do everything in their power to serve effectively. Readers who believe that the word is powerless without them will overshadow it. Once again, we find ourselves confronted by an apparent contradiction.

But it is only apparent. Another model — Jesus himself — can help us reconcile what seems to be a paradox. Jesus is the Word, and no one could deny that he applied himself to proclamation with total commitment. Yet there is no evidence that he forced the good news of God's love on anyone. He simply offered himself, to be rejected or accepted. "He emptied himself, taking the form of a slave, coming in human likeness" (Philippians 2:7). This looks like failure, but at no time was there any doubt that God's will would be accomplished in Jesus' suffering and death. It is precisely the passivity of the

passion that paved the way to redemption. It sounds strange, doesn't it, to speak of Jesus as passive? It also sounds strange to describe the role of the reader as passive. And yet it is, with the same results that Jesus achieved. Devoting ourselves completely to effective proclamation, we will achieve the best results by "taking the form of a slave" and thereby paving the way for God's word to achieve its end.

True service finds its roots in interior change and growth. It is the knowledge, faith and commitment of readers that will ultimately determine whether their ministry is effective. The skills of their art must be highly developed too, of course; their abilities as public communicators must be honed, improved and heightened. But the reflections that follow are born of the conviction that the most effective ministers of the word will be those who have allowed the ministry of proclamation to form them and transform them.

In the beginning was the Word,
and the Word was with God,
and the Word was God.
John 1:1

The Word

The word of God is not a thing, a book or a story. It is an act, a deed. The Hebrew makes this clear in *dabar,* a word that means "word" *and* "deed." Such a notion is not merely poetic, nor is it limited to the highly intuitive mode of thinking that we find in the Middle Eastern cultures from which our scriptures come. Contemporary language scholars in the West appreciate the richness of such a concept, too; they speak of words as actions of different kinds. Words are not just *things* that refer to other things; words *do* things. Two obvious examples

are "I baptize you" and "I forgive you." These are called "performative speech acts." They do not simply refer to an action; they actually effect the action they describe.

Reminders that the word is a deed are found throughout the Bible. The Ten Commandments are not merely tablets of stone; they are the wisdom of God inscribed on the hearts of the Israelite people and lived out in their lives. When the word of the Lord is entrusted to the prophets, they become walking, talking embodiments of it. And most precious of all for us Christians is the incarnate word, the word made flesh, the person of Jesus. This Anointed One is the word of God spoken from all eternity and born of a woman.

"Your faith has healed you," he said, and the woman was instantly cured. "Today salvation has come to this house," he said to Nicodemus, and a household of faith was born. "This day you will be with me in paradise," he said, and a thief was granted access to eternal life. "Neither do I condemn you," he said, and the adulterous woman was forgiven. "I do wish it," he said, and a leper was cleansed. "I am the true Bread come down from heaven," he said, and there were twelve baskets of bread left over. "Be opened," he said, and the deaf mute heard the words. "Father, into your hands I commend my spirit," he said, and thus consummated our redemption. We think of Jesus most vividly when we think of him as *being* the Word of God, not merely *speaking* it. Every word of Jesus was a saving deed; every deed of his was an incarnation of God's word.

We do well then as readers to remember that the word of God we proclaim is more than a mere record of God's intervention in history. It is a living and enabling continuance of that intervention. It is

God's activity in the world today. Readers at the liturgy are not merely teachers; they do not simply convey information. Rather, they enflesh the word through human speech. When they proclaim the word at the liturgy, Christ is present in the assembly, speaking the word that is his saving deed.

The effect of the proclaimed word

The liturgy makes the life, death and resurrection of Christ present to the assembled congregation in such a way that the assembly is disposed to live out the mysteries it witnesses and in which it participates. The liturgy effects what it signifies; that is, it makes the sacrificial action of Christ present and extends it throughout all time. The community that celebrates its salvation in the liturgy is built up by that very celebration and becomes a sign of the saving work of Christ continuing in the present.

The word proclaimed in the church's liturgy does what the liturgy itself does. It makes present the ongoing saving mercy and love of God. That is why the church can say of Christ, "He is present in his word since it is he himself who speaks when the holy scriptures are read in the church" (Vatican II, *Constitution on the Sacred Liturgy,* no. 7). The proclaimed word reveals to us the eternal activity of God in redeeming the world through Christ, the Word made flesh. The reader does not do this; the word does it. The analogy is clear: As God became flesh in Jesus — the Living Word — so that Word becomes flesh anew when the reader lifts it from the page. John the Evangelist puts it this way: The word became a living being [Jesus]. In perfect obedience to God, Jesus became the source of life for all the world. In the reader's obedience to God's command to tell the good news, the word is *proclaimed* through the ages as the source of life for all the world.

The parallel here is not particularly easy to grasp. It deserves meditation. But the implication of the parallel is clear: As readers we must surrender ourselves in service to the word in the full realization that *through* us, but *not because of* us, the word will become the source of life for all who have ears to hear it.

Is this merely an academic distinction? Not at all. When Jesus commissioned his apostles to preach the good news to all nations, they clearly understood that they had received something to give. The words they used were in part at least their own, but the news they proclaimed was God's, as revealed in Jesus. The news must have the medium of the human voice in order to be heard. But on its own the message achieves the end for which it was sent. We are the medium, not the message.

The point here is that a certain objectivity must characterize the ministry of reader. Otherwise, the reader will tend to overshadow the word with idiosyncratic interpretations or a mistaken sense of the ministry's purpose. Any attempt during the liturgy to "stage" the biblical text — to "act out" the text, to provide different "voices" in dialogue passages, to imitate the emotions recorded (rather than relate them) — will put the reader in the foreground at the expense of the word. Such practices betray a lack of confidence and faith in the word, and an understanding of proclamation that is far too didactic, pragmatic and "useful."

But mostly, such practices limit the universal appeal that the word must have to work its effect in lives and hearts very different from one another. For example, the reader who is dedicated to making every Bible text a reflection of the joy of being alive will hinder the word from being a comfort to those who are in mourning. The reader's purpose cannot be to make the word do something beyond what the liturgy does. The ministry of reader, along with the liturgy, celebrates the presence of Christ in our midst and does so without any ulterior motives.

People of the book

We can also speak of the word as "words." The medium of words, written and spoken, is one of the ways in which the word comes to us. It is not the only way, or even the most striking way, but it is an important and treasured way. For readers, the written words are the medium of their ministry. Language is the means by which, in human words, the divine word can be transmitted through the ages. Thus, the human words and the books that contain them are precious to us. They are a record of the living word intervening in history and are an important part of our tradition.

Christians have been called a "people of the book." The phrase suggests the important place the Bible has in our lives, for we consider it to be the written account of how our faith community understands the relationship between God and humanity. It is only recently, however, that Roman Catholics have begun again to see themselves as a "people of the book." Our emphasis for many centuries has been on being a "people of the table." That is, we exercised our faith and religion more vividly through

the sacraments, especially the "table of the Lord," the eucharist. This emphasis led us to define ourselves as different from other Christian communities that gathered regularly around the word but celebrated the eucharist with relative infrequency. The basis for this distinction is fading, however, as many Christian communities are developing a pattern of worship that includes the regular celebation of the eucharist. They are beginning to see themselves as "people of the book *and table.*"

For their part, Roman Catholics are growing in their appreciation of the word. While the Mass may be understood as being composed of two parts — the liturgy of the word and the liturgy of the eucharist — these distinctions may perpetuate the notion that the Mass is not one action but two. Even more misleading is the understandable but false notion that the liturgy of the word is (merely) preparation for the liturgy of the eucharist and is therefore secondary to it. It is fortunate that such notions are fading. For it is only when we see the liturgy of the Mass as one integral action that we will truly become "people of the book *and* table." Devotion to the ministry of the word and the celebration of the book will hasten the day when we see ourselves in this way.

Proclamation as ritual action

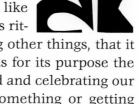

The proclamation of the word, like the liturgy of which it is part, is ritual action. That means, among other things, that it happens over and over and has for its purpose the gratuitous aims of praising God and celebrating our faith. It is not about giving something or getting something; it is about *doing something* — something very special — *for its own sake.* We engage in ritual action for much the same reason we play. It is done for itself and not for any practical or pragmatic reason. The liturgy of the word is not primarily an experience of teaching and being taught; it is a celebration of God being revealed in the proclamation just as much as the liturgy of the eucharist is a celebration of God being revealed in the actions of blessing, breaking and sharing.

Most people have no difficulty understanding the liturgy of the eucharist as ritual action. But many seem to see the liturgy of the word as an experience of being informed or instructed. The readings are perceived as lessons and the homily as didactic or instructional commentary on them. In truth, the proclamation of the word *is* the good news; it is not a lesson *about* the good news. The homily can perform a teaching function and is the proper place for it, but even the homily is not by definition an instruction. There are many legitimate purposes for the homily, only one of which is instruction. The homily may also inspire, encourage and celebrate.

In many Christian denominations a typical Sunday morning is divided into two parts: Sunday School and Worship. The worship service is preceded by a special kind of school that emphasizes Christian history, principles and doctrine. Catholic Christians often experience the same division at the Mass itself. Christian instruction is important, of course, and must be a part of our religious experience. We are disciples all our lives and that is why programs of "religious education" and "adult education" are essential in parish life. But the liturgy of the Mass is not the time or the place for such instruction. The true purpose of ritual action is not to inform but to form, not to educate but to celebrate. To the extent that the liturgy is perceived as primarily a learning experience, to that extent it is not ritual action.

How does all this affect the ministry of the reader? It defines the ministry on a much higher plane and so reveals how we are to go about it. Our ministry aims at celebrating the word of God and at doing so in such a way that we enhance that celebration in the hearts of those assembled. If we approach our ministry as teachers or catechists, we limit the word by forcing it into a specific time, space and situation that is too small to contain it. Again, readers serve the word; they do not make the word serve their predetermined purposes, however noble and well-intentioned.

■

Go, therefore, and make disciples of all nations . . .
teaching them to observe all
that I have commanded you.
Matthew 28:19 – 20

The Ministry

The ministry of the word is the responsibility of the church. As Bernard Cooke has noted, "'ministry of the word' can refer . . . to the Christian community's communication of the word of God to non-Christians or to the sharing of that word within the Christian church" (*Ministry to Word and Sacrament* [Philadelphia: Fortress Press, 1976], 324). Every baptized Christian is entrusted with the obligation to spread the news that God has a plan for the world and that this plan excludes no one. No matter how much we categorize this duty

Make
disciples of
all nations.
teaching them
to observe
all that
I have
commanded
you

or assign it in special ways to particular persons, the truth remains: The entire church, and every member, is a minister of the word to the world. It is important to remember this as we examine one very particular form of the ministry of the word — that of the reader at the liturgy.

Since the Second Vatican Council, the presence and role of the reader in the Roman Catholic liturgy has undergone much development. Altar servers, choir members and cantors have had an active liturgical presence in some form for centuries. But the lay reader is relatively new to us. Understandably, we have seen a variety of ways in which this new role has been exercised, and we have had to discover the most effective way for readers to fulfill their ministry. And now, after nearly 30 years of experience, we are in a position to define the ministry more clearly than ever.

Defining the reader's ministry

Good ministry is always, by nature, self-effacing, for its aim is the good of another; the focus of good ministry is always upon those being ministered to. Let us make the important point, then, that the focus of the reader's proclamation is on the assembly. The reader ministers to the assembly by proclaiming over and over the good news that is the word of God in sacred scripture. This is done most effectively when the assembly is seen as the church in miniature. That means that in any given assembly, there will be a wide variety of concerns, needs and degrees of receptivity.

The sensitive reader who understands the universality of the word knows that a degree of restraint and objectivity must be exercised in this ministry. Within the body of hearers will be some who are at peace, some who are tortured by doubts, some who are grieving, some who are profoundly happy, and so on. The word being proclaimed is for all and will be received according to each hearer's state in life. Thus, the reader must proclaim the word in such a way that it is accessible to a very diverse group.

The tendency we sometimes hear in readers to make the text individualistic or to shade it with their own personal application betrays an insufficient degree of objectivity and of sensitivity to the assembly's diverse needs. More fundamentally, it indicates a view of liturgy and proclamation that is too rational and practical, one that has veered away from understanding that the whole point of the liturgy is the gratuitous praise of God and the celebration of the life of faith.

Problem-solving is not the aim of the reader's proclamation of the word, just as it is not the aim of the liturgy. The proclamation of the word, like the liturgy itself, is oriented toward something broader — and ultimately more fulfilling — than the narrow and variable confines of problem-solving. In fact, the more our proclamation participates in the broader celebratory nature of the liturgy, the more apt it is to address a variety of hearers and dispose them toward living their lives based on the word. Again, the fundamental conviction that we serve the word — and not the reverse — is what guarantees that our proclamation will be genuine ministry.

Because our ministry as readers takes place within the context of the liturgy, it is ritual ministry. That is, its purpose is to make present to the assembled worshipers the realities they believe in. As Vatican II teaches us, "the works performed by God in the

history of salvation show forth and bear out the doctrine and realities signified by the words; the words, for their part, proclaim the works, and bring to light the mystery they contain" (*Dogmatic Constitution on Divine Revelation* [*Dei Verbum*], no. 2).

The reader formation program

For a variety of reasons (all of them quite practical) formation programs for readers are concerned more often with public speaking skills than with formation unto ministry. It is true, of course, that these kinds of skills are extremely important, even most important, pragmatically speaking. If the reader cannot be heard and cannot be understood, all else is for naught. Nevertheless, what really comes first in the order of importance is that potential readers be instilled with a thorough understanding of the nature of the word of God and with a profound respect and love for it. To this must be added a clear understanding of the purpose of the proclamation of scripture in the context of ritual celebration.

None of this can be accomplished in a weekend workshop or in a book like this one. It can be accomplished only in an on-going program that includes study of the scriptures, study of the nature of the church, study of the liturgy and its purpose, and a thorough review of salvation history as understood and taught by the church. A truly effective program will also include a review of the structure and plan of the Lectionary as well as of the various kinds of literature found in the Bible. Finally, it will include instruction and coaching in effective public reading skills by someone who understands the uniqueness of this art as it is applied to the proclamation of the word of God at the liturgy.

After 30 years of working with the teachings of Vatican II, we are now in a position to bring a great deal of knowledge and experience to bear upon our understanding of the ministry of the reader. It is time to define the ministry and its requirements in more specific terms. With an accurate understanding of the importance and dignity of the reader's ministry, we will expect from readers no less than we expect from presiders, deacons, musicians and preachers — all of whom undergo extensive formation for their ministries.

It is no longer permissible or necessary simply to assign this ministry to a dozen (or five dozen) willing souls who are reasonably good public speakers and thus consider the office of reader in the parish covered. To do so is to ensure that the inadequate proclamations we hear today will continue and that the liturgy of the word will not be the powerful ritual experience the church intends it to be. Proclamation of the word will continue to be identified as catechesis and propaganda rather than as a ritual celebration that makes our beliefs present. The principle is neatly packaged in the Latin formula *lex orandi, lex credendi:* As we pray and worship, so will we believe.

■

A lamp to my feet is your word,
a light to my path.
Psalm 119:105

The Reader

The reader is called from among the People of God to proclaim the word of God in the midst of the worshiping assembly. The presumption must be that the men and women who take on the ministry of reader are of good faith, eager to serve their fellow Christians and willing to engage in ongoing formation. The presumption must not be that such people are especially pious, exceptionally gifted or particularly skilled in public communication techniques. Certain basic abilities are presumed, and these are discussed in other resource

A LAMP UNTO MY FEET IS YOUR WORD

books available to readers. Special skills related to certain professions (public speakers, broadcasters, actors) do not automatically qualify someone to proclaim the scriptrues during the liturgy — where the purpose is quite different. The desire to serve as a reader is welcome but does not automatically qualify one for the ministry. The proclamation of the word is an awesome responsibility that is imposed by the church. It is not every Christian's right, for not every Christian is capable of this ministry.

Because the office of reader is relatively new in our post – Vatican II church, we are only now beginning to understand just how important it is and how much the effectiveness of the liturgy depends upon it. Some current practices, therefore, are bound to fall away when we come to realize that they compromise the ministry of reader. The following are some examples.

Impromptu readers It happens sometimes that a member of the congregation is chosen, almost at random, to proclaim the scripture readings at Mass. This practice betrays a woeful lack of understanding of what proclaiming the readings at Mass involves — indeed, a lack of appreciation for the word of God. It would be unthinkable to choose our musicians, catechists, deacons or altar servers at random from among people unformed in these ministries. Why would we so choose a reader? Or consider another situation: In assembling the members of my wedding party, I decide that it would be nice if my sister read one of the readings at the nuptial Mass. Unless my sister normally serves as a reader in the parish, I should be prepared to hear that this ministry is reserved to those who are formed in it.

Very young readers It is not uncommon to see young, even pre-teen children serve as readers at

Mass, especially at Masses for children or on special occasions such as liturgies that are part of grade school or high school graduation ceremonies. It is difficult to see how a child could be expected to proclaim the word of God with sufficient understanding and skill. What such a practice reveals is a mistaken set of expectations. The effect may be charming, endearing and even touching; but clearly the reader has been brought into the foreground at the expense of the word. In any case, our expectations of the proclaimed word must go beyond the charming and touching.

Too many readers   Sometimes we find the principle of "more is better" working against the quality of liturgical proclamation. Though it may seem best to have a great number of readers in a parish — so that more people have the opportunity to exercise this ministry and the work load is lightened — some reflection reveals that this has a negative side. To be effective, ministers of the word need to exercise their ministry on a fairly regular basis. At least once a month would seem to be the minimum. If the ministry falls to them only two or three Sundays a year, readers will find their skills suffering from infrequent use. But scheduling need not be on a weekly or monthly basis. Concentrated experience might compensate for less frequent experience if readers were to be assigned for a liturgical season (all of Lent, all of Advent, half of Ordinary Time).

Most significantly, the degree of formation and education that is necessary for truly effective ministry would preclude the involvement of great numbers of readers in any given parish. The reader "breaks open the word" for us, just as the presider at Mass "breaks the bread" for us. To do so effectively requires extensive preparation, practice and

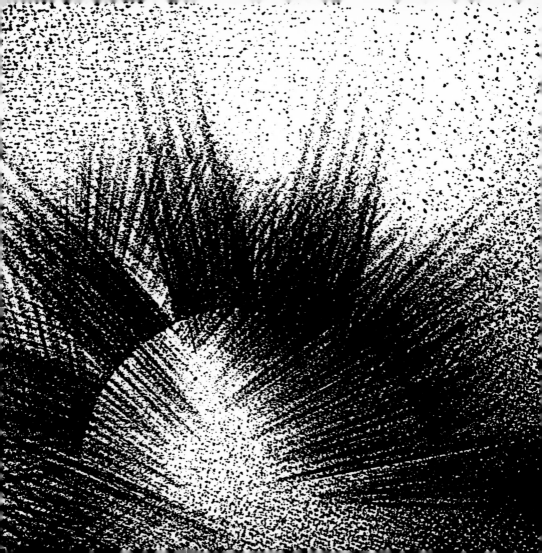

devotion to the task. Readers who are most effective realize that they are part of a team and that their function takes place in the context of liturgical celebration. They make it clear to us that the word of God is alive with power, deserving our rapt attention. Through the word, the reader is truly a minister: encouraging, rebuking and consoling us, inspiring us and urging us on toward greater wisdom and insight into the ways of God. What do readers do? In their proclamation, the promises of God are fulfilled in our hearing.

Basic abilities v. learned skills

Much about the ministry of reader can be learned; and many of the communication skills required for the ministry can be acquired. But certain native abilities must also be present in the person who is chosen to proclaim the word.

Not everyone has the necessary vocal quality or power, even with the help of amplification, to perform this service effectively. Not everyone will be able to deal with the special nature of the language of the scriptures. And there may be some who approach this ministry with convictions that are contrary to what it requires — for example, seeing no distinction between dramatic interpretation and liturgical proclamation. On the other hand, there is no reason to exclude those who are physically handicapped if their condition has no direct effect on their potential as a reader. One of the finest readers I know is one of my former students who is almost totally blind. He makes Braille copies of the readings, and he proclaims them with exceptional power and conviction.

If a potential reader possesses the basic abilities required for public communication, the next thing to look for is the desire and willingness to participate in an extended formation program. This will include studying sacred scripture, liturgy, literary forms, the plan of the Lectionary and the nature of the church. Such a list is daunting, but nothing on it can be omitted without jeopardizing the reader's effectiveness. Formation into the ministry of reader is a serious, exciting and extensive undertaking. Until it is understood as such, the proclamation of the word of God at the liturgy will not achieve its full purpose. None of these areas of study is beyond the competence of a person with average intelligence, a lively faith and the eagerness to serve. And resources for study in all these areas are readily available.

The ministry's effect on the reader

How does this ministry affect the minister? Readers who form themselves into their ministry may find their experience of liturgy and Christian life changed. In studying the scriptures and discovering meanings far beyond the literal and scientific, many readers will come to know Jesus as being very different from what they were taught as children. They will discover the living Jesus, the resurrected Christ, who pervades every time and place — the Christ whose words, as he himself said, "are spirit and life." Readers will be fascinated to come to know the Jesus of the Gospel of Matthew and see how different he is from the Jesus of the gospels of Mark, Luke and John.

In learning the particular view of each gospel writer, the unique theology of Paul, and the power and sweep of the Hebrew Scriptures, readers will begin to see something of the constancy and the mercy of God's persistent pursuit of the world in love. They will learn that even the so-called historical books of the Bible are primarily works of theology, not science. In short, they will see that sacred scripture is the community's understanding of how God has interacted with it.

In their study of liturgy, well-formed readers will begin to appreciate the nature and power of ritual celebration and will be able to distinguish celebration and prayer from education and propaganda. In a new discovery of what the Sunday assembly has gathered to do, the reader will know that liturgical proclamation is more enabling than it is instructive, more celebration than it is information, more concerned with making Christ present in the assembly than it is with studying his life and commands.

In their study of the communication skills needed for proclamation, readers will learn the difference between dramatic reading and ritual proclamation, between re-enacting the text and re-presenting it. They will bring to bear all the skills of the public communicator, but for the purpose of celebrating the life of faith, not directly for teaching the assembly how to live that life.

Public recognition of the reader

Relatively few parishes formally recognize those who are involved in the ministry of reader with a blessing or a ceremony of installation. This need not be the case, however, because of the resources available that make such recognition possible. The *Book of Blessings,* for example, contains an "Order for the Blessing of Readers." Of course the purpose of such a ritual is not so much to honor the minister but to give public recognition to the importance of the ministry and prayerful support to the ministers — just as we do for communion ministers, altar servers, ministers of music, and those in the orders of deacon, presbyter and bishop. Using the "Order for the Blessing of Readers" during a parish Sunday Mass can also be a reminder to the assembly of the significance of the ministry of reader for the church's liturgical life.

■

Your word, O LORD, endures forever;
it is firm as the heavens.
Psalm 119:89

The Book

Sacred scripture, the Bible, is a precious written legacy handed down to us from our ancestors. It does not contain all of God's word, but it does contain accounts of how the earliest faith communities understood God's interaction with them. The inspired writings of the Bible speak of God's relationship with humanity from the time of Abraham, "our father in faith," through the early history of Israel and continuing through the first years of Christianity.

The Bible's origins, like those of our faith itself, are found in the countries and cultures of what we now call the Middle East. We can never lose sight of the differences that exist between our culture and those of this part of the world. The Middle Eastern mentality is very different from our own; it is more intuitive, more poetic and more visionary. The rationalism of Western civilization has touched all of us in some way and can lead us into a reading of the Bible texts that is too literal, too scientific, too unimaginative. Thankfully, biblical scholarship abounds and is easily available. Those who would be readers must avail themselves of it, lest their understanding of biblical texts be naive or simplistic.

As an example of how important it is to consider the cultural roots of our Bible texts, consider the following. When Jesus tells us to "offer no resistance to injury" and to "turn the other cheek," he is employing very dramatic language to tell us how different we must become in order to follow him. A literal interpretation of this advice would be inconceivable to Middle Eastern listeners. They would see in Jesus' words the challenge to change, to be radically different — but they would not for a moment think they were being asked to tolerate deliberate physical abuse.

Discovering and communicating the *meaning* of sacred scripture is not easy; we need to rely on more than the words themselves. Those who devote their lives to the study of the Bible are our greatest helpers in this regard. They have mastered the original languages of the Bible and have studied the cultures of the people among whom the scripture were born. Their scholarship enables us to read the Bible in all its richness and complexity — and to avoid literal interpretations that miss the deeper meanings revealed through the subtleties and nuances peculiar to every language, time and place.

The language of the Bible

All of sacred scripture is written in exalted language. The best translations preserve not only the meaning but also the tone of the original text. Readers who feel obliged to recast the biblical texts in their own words — to achieve a more contemporary idiom — are more concerned with imparting information than with enhancing worship and celebration. Their intentions may be quite noble: to make the Bible warmer, more intimate, more accessible, more relevant. However, such practices stem from a lack of understanding of liturgical proclamation, indeed, of liturgy itself, for they emphasize the didactic and the pragmatic at the expense of the gratuitous and celebratory. The effect is to trivialize both the text and the hearer.

The most immediate message given by such practices is that the word is insufficient on its own and that the assembly needs to be "talked down to." Inevitably, this draws attention to the reader and away from the reading. The ultimate test to use here is based on the principle of "foregrounding." Whatever we do to put the sacred text into the foreground of the assembly's attention serves the purpose of liturgical proclamation. Whatever we do that places the reader, the language of the text or the style of delivery into the foreground compromises that purpose.

Literary genres

The Bible contains many different kinds of literature: narratives (stories), poems, sermons, hymns, sayings, and so on. Notice the great difference between these selections from the readings for the Second Sunday of Advent (Year C):

> Up, Jerusalem! stand upon the heights;
>   look to the east and see your children
> Gathered from the east and the west
>   at the word of the Holy One,
>   rejoicing that they are remembered by God.

First Reading — Baruch 5:5

I give thanks to my God at every
   remembrance of you,
praying always with joy
in my every prayer for all of you,
because of your partnership for the gospel
from the first day until now.

Second Reading — Philippians 1:3-5

In the fifteenth year of the reign of
   Tiberius Caesar,
when Pontius Pilate was governor of Judea,
and Herod was tetrarch of Galilee,
and his brother Philip
tetrarch of the region of Ituraea and
   Trachonitis,
and Lysanias was tetrarch of Abilene,
during the high priesthood of Annas
   and Caiphas,

the word of God came to John the son
of Zechariah in the desert.

Gospel — Luke 3:1-2

In the first reading we encounter pure poetry, exhorting the listener to joy. In the second reading we listen in on a letter from a pastor telling his flock how much he loves them and delights in their acceptance of the good news. In the gospel reading we are presented with what can be called a "ritual narrative," a long list of historical references that sets the scene for a story, in this case, the story of the appearance of John the Baptist. The purpose of the ritual beginning is far more than mere historical scene-setting. It intends to contrast the coming of the Messiah (and his spiritual kingdom) with the earthly rulership of his contemporaries.

There is a very important reason for recognizing and respecting the different literary styles that appear in the Bible: The writer's message is told in a certain way — a literary form — because the writer is making a certain point. The choice of style is not arbitrary. A classic example, of course, is the poetry of Genesis in the accounts of creation. If we forget that the writer's purpose is to show that God is the origin and the sustaining power of all that exists, we could repeat a mistake that has been made down through the ages, namely, interpreting the poetic text literally. Knowing that there are two accounts of creation in Genesis (1:1 — 2:4 and 2:5 — 2:25) and that they do not agree with each other should be enough to convince us that the authors were not concerned with scientific data. Poetry is usually not the style of choice for empirical scientists.

The many parables told by Jesus are each concerned with the teaching of a spiritual or moral lesson. If we get lost in the details of a parable, we will surely miss its larger purpose. Events that are described in miraculous terms (such as the feeding of the multitude with five loaves and two fishes) may or may not be interpreted as "breaking the laws of nature." But the larger point being made by the author must not be missed in any case: God's promises and provident love will not be thwarted, either by natural or supernatural agents.

The same principle applies to the many literary devices employed in the Bible. Parallelism, alliteration and onomatopoeia are features of some texts that will take care of themselves in the mouth of a careful, attentive and knowledgeable reader. They are not so elusive that we have to draw special attention to them. Literary devices, after all, are simply ways to make an idea or message more memorable. If they draw attention to themselves and away from the message, they are ineffective.

Parallelism is the most common literary device found in the Hebrew Scriptures. Here is an example from the first reading on the Third Sunday in Ordinary Time (Year A). Notice how each line is echoed in, expanded upon, or mirrored by the line that follows. The experienced reader knows how to proclaim such texts so that the parallelism makes the message more memorable. A great deal of sensitivity to language, as well as extensive practice, is required before this kind of Bible poetry will work its intended effect.

> The people who walked in darkness
> have seen a great light;

Upon those who dwelt in the land of gloom
  a light has shone.
You have brought them abundant joy
  and great rejoicing.
As they rejoice before you as at the harvest,
  as men make merry when dividing spoils.
For the yoke that burdened them,
  the pole on their shoulder,
And the rod of their taskmaster
  you have smashed, as on the day of Midian.

Isaiah 9:2-4

Inclusive language

There is one contemporary issue
regarding biblical texts that deserves

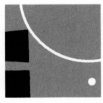

very special attention: inclusive language. Some translations of the Bible still lag behind our sensitivity to language that implies the exclusion of women or a prejudice against certain peoples. Progress is being made in this regard. And we must further it. The *New Revised Standard Version* is a translation of the Bible that carefully addresses the inclusive language issue with regard to human beings — though it does not deal with the Bible's almost exclusive use of masculine forms referring to God. The same is true of the *Revised New American Bible.* It too recasts the texts to make them inclusive with regard to human beings but maintains language predominantly masculine in referring to God.

It is a serious mistake for us to oversimplify the inclusive language issue. Readers who revise the texts blithely are exceeding both their authority and their expertise. They must avail themselves of credible scholarship on this issue, and when faced with difficult situations, they must strive for a balance between drawing too much attention to the issue itself (and therefore away from the message of the text) and offending the assembly with language that excludes many of them.

To keep our wits about us in the midst of the inclusive language issue, there are several things we need to remember. First, the English language is, by its very nature, preferential toward the masculine form. Second, both testaments of the Bible were composed in cultures that were strongly patriarchal, which explains, in part at least, why the masculine form is almost always used in reference to God. The exceptions prove the rule. Third, most existing English translations, themselves being culture-bound, reflect the bias inherent in the English language — often to the point of actually distorting the original. The classic and often-quoted example is the translation of the Greek word *anthropoi* as "men," when in fact it means "human beings."

The experience of readers where this issue is concerned may be quite dramatic. They may be approached by a member of the assembly and admonished for changing the text as it appears in the missalette. In such instances the presumption must be that the concerned worshiper is genuinely worried about a tendency to treat the sacred texts frivolously or disrespectfully. It is a valid concern. But it must be balanced by an awareness that many in the assembly feel disenfranchised by language that excludes them — and that no translation that does so is adequate.

Until a lectionary is published that uses an inclusive language translation of the Bible, readers will have to continue to make prudential judgments —

ideally in concert with the parish liturgy team — on whether or not to edit the Lectionary texts to make them inclusive. Readers will certainly be confronted with situations in which the use of exclusive language would be very insensitive and unkind. On the other hand, there will be situations in which the use of inclusive language (by editing the text) would cause grave concern and overshadow the larger purpose of proclaiming the word.

■

My word . . . shall not return to me void, but shall do my will, achieving the end for which I sent it.

Isaiah 55:11

The Community

Consider the special environment in which the reader's ministry takes place. Consider also how much our ministry depends on its environment to be effective. We minister in the midst of the assembly — that particular group of God's people that has come together to celebrate and renew the gift of faith. What a wonderful mixture of people it is that comes together at the liturgy — and all for the purpose of celebrating mutual love and unity of faith!

MY WORD SHALL NOT RETURN THREAD

In such gatherings, everything depends on everything else if the purpose of the gathering is to be fulfilled. That is why ministers of the word must see themselves as part of a team: assembly, servers, presider, maintenance engineers, communion ministers, ushers, cantors, musicians, sacristans, decorators — and the list is still not complete. Each of these serves one common goal: to provide a setting in which faith can celebrate itself and grow.

The practical considerations are legion: the environment, art and furnishings, the public address system, the lighting, the liturgical books, the worship aids, the seating of latecomers, and so on. The needs will differ from assembly to assembly and according to each situation, but the point is that such things must be taken into account, for they do affect the celebration of the word — for good or for ill. Reader formation programs cannot neglect these practical considerations, for they have direct bearing on the effectiveness of the word as proclaimed in the liturgical setting.

The spoken word as sacrament

The proclamation of the word is a sacramental act. It has all the features of sacred ritual action, whose purpose is to effect what it signifies. Like a sacrament, it involves human contact through speech, sound and hearing. In more solemn celebrations it is accompanied by song, acclamation and incense. Every reading is begun and concluded with a ritual dialogue. "A reading from . . . " is akin to "Hear ye, hear ye!" And "The word of the Lord!" is a trumpet call to assent to the good news still ringing in our ears. It is a performative use of language: The word that proclaims the presence of God in our midst effects the presence of God in our midst. Vatican II said it most clearly in the Constitution on the Sacred Liturgy (no. 7): ". . . it is [Christ] himself who speaks when the holy Scriptures are read in the Church." Our natural response to the one who speaks is to listen, not to read along.

The issue of missalettes deserves special mention because it raises a significant concern. There should be no need or desire on the part of the assembly to use a printed text of the readings. (The obvious exception is for the hearing impaired.) The sacramental nature of the act of proclamation — bringing the printed word to life through the human voice — is completed by the act of hearing the word proclaimed. Those who say that they get more out of the text by reading along with the reader have probably not experienced truly effective readers. Or perhaps they view the word of God as a history lesson or code of conduct rather than as a celebration of God's presence. In either case, the emphasis is on *information* rather than *formation.* And while we are certainly informed by the word, the liturgical proclamation of it is a *formative* experience more than an *informative* one.

It is an observable fact that in assemblies served by excellent readers, the use of missalettes declines sharply. Whatever needs to be done in a practical way to enhance the experience of hearing the word proclaimed well (reader formation, public address system, building acoustics) should be attended to vigorously. Anything less than scrupulous attention to these considerations sends out the message that the liturgy is not worth all the work involved in celebrating it well.

Ritual dialogue

Every Lectionary reading begins and ends with a ritual dialogue with 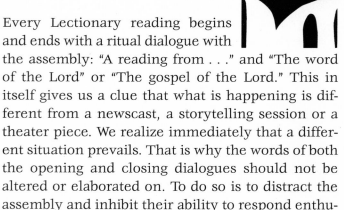 the assembly: "A reading from . . ." and "The word of the Lord" or "The gospel of the Lord." This in itself gives us a clue that what is happening is different from a newscast, a storytelling session or a theater piece. We realize immediately that a different situation prevails. That is why the words of both the opening and closing dialogues should not be altered or elaborated on. To do so is to distract the assembly and inhibit their ability to respond enthusiastically. For example, to end with something like, "And this, my brothers and sisters, is the word of the Lord," is to invoke a relationship that is irrelevant at this point in the liturgy and to make the assembly's response less spontaneous.

In 1993, the church directed that the reader's half of the closing dialogue be shortened from "This is the word of the Lord" to "The word of the Lord." Gospel readers announce, "The gospel of the Lord." The change is an improvement. Much of the language we use in the liturgy is special and is different from everyday language because liturgy is different from everyday activities. Liturgy is, above all else, something we do, not something we "talk." The kind of language we use in liturgy is very often language that does something, not language that tells something.

Language specialists know well that language has more than one purpose: We can use it to convey information ("The opening hymn is on page 228") or to accomplish an action ("I absolve you from

your sins"). Sometimes the words we use have little to do with the meaning we want to convey. For example, when we are being introduced to someone and we say "How do you do?" we don't expect our new acquaintance to actually answer the question! If someone responds with "How do I do what?" we might wonder whether the meeting is a happy one. "How do you do?" is an accepted ritual expression that doesn't literally mean "How do you do?" It is courteous behavior, not a literal question.

So what is the difference between "This is the word of the Lord" and "The word of the Lord"? A great deal! From a grammatical point of view, "This" (a demonstrative pronoun) and "is" (a verb) make the sentence more like the language we use to tell something rather than to do something. At this point in the liturgy, however, we are *doing* something — celebrating the word of God as it still rings in our ears. In contrast to "This is . . ." "The word of the Lord!" is more like a trumpet blast than a piece of information. It is the kind of language we use when we want our words to mean more than meets the ear. Our response is also an exalted piece of ritual language: "Thanks be to God."

There are other examples of this in the liturgy. The example most like "The word of the Lord" is what we hear when we receive communion: "The Body of Christ" and "The Blood of Christ." The communion minister is not simply telling us what we are receiving ("This is the Body of Christ" or "This is the Blood of Christ"). No, the minister is *doing* something here — celebrating the faith you have in this great sacrament. And so are you when you reply "Amen."

So, this little change in the liturgy is not so little after all. It reminds us that liturgy is neither a classroom nor a gathering where people *tell* each other things they already know. It is a community that *does* something very special. And the language that is used echoes the community's purpose for being there.

The Lectionary

The Lectionary is a liturgical book containing selections from the Bible arranged for proclamation according to the liturgical year. It is clearly a precious article; it is worthy of respect, honor and even enthronement. It is to be ornately and beautifully bound, carried high in processions, incensed, kissed, and, in short, shown every sign of veneration. It is an important signal to the members of the assembly whenever they witness the reverence shown to the Lectionary. They perceive, without being told, that the word of God is revered even in the form of a printed volume. However, another signal is given when the Lectionary is not treated with respect. It is not uncommon to see the Lectionary carried high in procession and then placed on the floor next to the reader's seat until it is needed. The contradictory messages should shake us into greater sensitivity.

The book itself is worthy of great reverence, but once the word has been enfleshed by the human voice, we have something greater to revere: the word enfleshed by the human voice and still ringing in our ears. In some places the custom has developed that the reader elevates the book while announcing "The word of the Lord" or "The gospel of the Lord." But such a practice misses an opportunity to communicate something of the sacramentality of the *spoken* word.

To draw attention to the book at this point is to draw attention away from the word enfleshed by the human minister. Would it not be better to establish firm eye contact with the assembly and then speak the words "The word of the Lord" or "The gospel of the Lord" with real conviction? The implication is: "What I have just read to you — what is still resounding in your ears — is the word of the Lord, once more enlivened by human sharing."

Individual v. group preparation

Most readers usually find themselves preparing for their ministry in the privacy of their homes. It is worth trying, however, to have them gather as a group for some preparations, such as study of the scriptures and of the liturgy, and for mutual critiques. There is merit in the readers of a parish seeing themselves as a team, encouraging each other toward more effective ministry. One gets the impression that most readers lead rather isolated lives in their preparation for proclaiming the word. There are communities, however, where readers gather regularly for scripture studies, liturgy planning and workshops presented by persons equipped to further their formation. Invariably, readers who have the advantage of a supportive group in their ongoing formation find their ministry not only more rewarding, but also more effective.

■

The Lord GOD has given me a well-trained tongue,
That I may know how to speak to the weary
a word that will rouse them.

Isaiah 50:4

Looking Back . . .
and Ahead

The word proclaimed at the liturgy will achieve its purpose when we are led into the celebration of Christ's presence. Yes, the word of God does something: It makes the transforming presence of Christ real to us. Hearing the scriptures actually transforms us and makes us holy. Recall the well-known saying of Jesus, "Happy are those who hear the word of God and keep it." The very act of hearing the word is part of the sanctifying process. *Hearing* the word is not only the prelude to keeping it but is also part of the very act of keeping

THE LORD HAS GIVEN
ME A WELL TRAINED
TONGUE
THAT I MAY KNOW
HOW TO SPEAK
TO THE WEARY A WORD
THAT WILL ROUSE
THEM

it! The reader's ultimate purpose is to enable the People of God to "hear the word of God and keep it."

I began these reflections with three personal experiences of hearing the word over a span of 20 years. Recall the fundamentalist preacher who succeeded so well in making me feel the presence of God, albeit a God very different from the one I know now. Though his approach to proclaiming the word now seems inadequate to me (for it sought not so much to celebrate the word of God as to dictate my behavior), I nevertheless remember with great vividness and admiration his fervor, his energy and his obvious sincerity; there was nothing offhanded or desultory about his faith or his proclamation. Obviously, his influence on me has endured to this day. Though it is difficult to say precisely how he did so, this minister of the word enabled me to celebrate the reality of God, alive and vigorously present in the lives of my fellow Christians assembled for worship. Surely the preacher's own transformation in Jesus explains the effectiveness of his ministry.

The very different experience of Catholic monastic liturgy in the days before Vatican II is also very much alive in me. The proclamation of the word in that milieu left no room for doubt regarding the seriousness and significance of our worship. The sheer weight, complexity and formality of that polychromatic setting of the word made it unforgettable and moving. There was never any danger of judging this style of proclamation excessively didactic or pragmatic. It was the essence of gratuitous praise. And yet there seemed such a separation between my daily life and my liturgical life that the two could not mesh very easily. On the other hand, when I think today of what ritual proclamation of the word often seems to lack, I find myself remembering the enormous care, devotion and sacredness accorded the word in those liturgies.

The opposite extreme seems to apply to my experience in the 1970s. The young man who more or less translated the scripture reading into his own personal experience and proclaimed it with such emotional intensity showed me just how "real" the word can be in individual lives. The problem, though, is that an experience of the word so personal and so individual could not encompass the diversity of the assembly, much less the cosmic dimension of a God who must always be, by definition, in great part unknowable. The proclaimed word in this context was simply too small, too constricted. The reader's youthful vigor and personal faith were compelling, but did not supply the necessary breadth and objectivity. Liturgical proclamation foregrounds the universal experience of the assembly, not the personal experience of the minister.

**The Lord God has given me
  a well-trained tongue
That I may know how
  to speak to the weary**

The title of this book was carefully chosen. The passage from Isaiah from which it is drawn (50:4) includes both aspects of the reader's ministry. A well-trained tongue is necessary for anyone who wishes to speak effectively for God and rouse the people of God from their weariness. And the words proclaimed by the tongue must come from a heart formed and transformed by a familiarity with the word of God, an acute awareness of the purpose of liturgy and ministry, and a profound sensitivity to the sufferings of the weary.

The minister of the word who has been so transformed knows that the objective at hand is not primarily to teach or to tell, to instruct or to guide, or to compel or cajole. No, it is to stand in the midst of the assembly with integrity and faith and *proclaim* the word that renews the presence of the saving God. That is the word that will rouse them.

■

Publishers' addresses can be found at the end of this section.

Texts and commentaries

Manual para proclamadores de la palabra. Spanish language version of the *Workbook for Lectors and Gospel Readers.* It contains Sunday readings, commentaries and notes on proclamation. Liturgy Training Publications.

Mulligan, Frank J. *Reading at Mass: Guidelines for the Lector.* Brief commentary and hints for proclamation for all Sunday readings. The Liturgical Press, 1990.

Ramshaw, Gail. *Richer Fare: Reflections on the Sunday Readings.* Pueblo, 1990.

Workbook for Lectors and Gospel Readers. An annual publication containing the year's Sunday readings with commentary and suggestions for effective proclamation. Liturgy Training Publications.

Audio and Video Tapes

Lector Training Program: This is the Word of the Lord.
 Three audiocassettes, booklet and worksheet.
 Liturgy Training Publications, 1988.
Proclaiming the Word: Formation for Readers in the
 Liturgy. Foundational and formational 40-minute
 video for new as well as experienced readers.
 Liturgy Training Publications, 1994.
The Word of the Lord: The Liturgy of the Word. Readers,
 preachers and parishioners speak of their hopes
 for the liturgy of the word in this 30-minute video.
 Liturgy Training Publications, 1995.

Other resources of interest to readers

At Home With the Word. Liturgy Training Publications.
Keifer, Ralph. *To Hear and Proclaim: Introduction to*
 the Lectionary for Mass. Pastoral Press, 1983.

LaVerdiere, Eugene. *Dining in the Kingdom of God: The Origins of the Eucharist According to Luke.* Liturgy Training Publications, 1994.

Lectionary for Mass: Introduction. Liturgy Documentary Series 1. United States Catholic Conference, 1982.

Lonergan, Ray. *A Well-Trained Tongue: A Workbook for Lectors.* Liturgy Training Publications, 1982.

National Conference of Catholic Bishops. *Proclaim the Word: Lectionary for Mass.* Liturgy Study Text Series 8. United States Catholic Conference, 1982.

Wallace, James. *The Ministry of Lectors.* The Liturgical Press, 1981.

Publishers

The Liturgical Press
Pueblo Books
P.O. Box 7500
Collegeville MN 56321
1-800-858-5450

Liturgy Training Publications
1800 North Hermitage Avenue
Chicago IL 60622-1101
1-800-933-1800

The Pastoral Press
225 Sheridan Street, NW
Washington DC 20011
202-723-1254

United States Catholic Conference
Office for Publishing and Promotional Services
3211 Fourth Street, NE
Washington DC 20017